THIS BOOK BELONGS TO

BREATHE

devotions to quiet the soul

Ellie Claire
Hachette Book Group
1290 Avenue of the Americas, New York, NY 10104
ellieclaire.com

First Edition: October 2019

Ellie Claire is a division of Hachette Book Group, Inc. The Ellie Claire name and logo are trademarks of Hachette Book Group, Inc.

The publisher is not responsible for websites (or their content) that are not owned by the publisher.

Stock or custom editions of Ellie Claire titles may be purchased in bulk for educational, business, ministry, fundraising, or sales promotional use. For information, please e-mail info@EllieClaire.com

Interior design and typesetting by Bart Dawson

Library of Congress Cataloging-in-Publication Data has been applied for.

ISBN: 9781546014393 (hardcover)

Printed in China

RRD

10 9 8 7 6 5 4 3 2 1

THANK YOU TO OUR CONTRIBUTORS:

Leigh Powers

Kristel Acevedo

Victoria Duerstock

Aleah Marsden

Carol Reid

Trisha Mugo

Lawrence Wilson

Evelyn Wells

Kimberly Shumate

Jeannie Waters

Michelle Cox

Paula Moldenhauer

Carlton Hughes

Donna Huisjen

Danetta Kellar

Ramona Richards

Michelle Adams

Linda Gilden

Jeanette Hanscome

Lauren Craft

Leslie McKee

Edie Melson

Melissa Collier

Pauline Hylton

Jane Reed

JoHannah Rearden

Lucinda Secrest McDowell

Penny Hunt

INHALE.

EXHALE.

JUST BREATHE

The eternal God is your dwelling place,
and underneath are the everlasting arms.

DEUTERONOMY 33:27 ESV

Life is busy and fast-paced, whether it's because you're a mom keeping up with energetic children or you have a job that requires you to be always on the move. You may be wondering when life will slow down so you can rest. But sometimes stopping just isn't an option and the chaos can be overwhelming. Life doesn't always slow down when we want or need it to.

When we can't stop the commotion we can stop to take a breath in the middle of the chaos. We can close our eyes and remember Who is holding us.

God has never left us, and the disarray we are experiencing is no surprise to Him. His arms are everlasting and in them we find security. We don't have to fear that the chaos will consume us, because He is protecting us.

Do not fear, because He has overcome the world, and that includes the chaos surrounding you right now. Dwell in Him.

* * * * * * * * * *

Dear Father, even when I feel like I am drowning,
You are always holding me. Thank You for Your loving arms
that always protect me from the chaos of life.

TRUST IN THE GOOD TIMES

The LORD is good to all;
he has compassion on all he has made.
PSALM 145:9 NIV

Sometimes life is going incredibly well. You don't have a care in the world because everything is "coming up roses." But then anxiety starts creeping in. You think that life can't possibly be this good and you begin to fear that soon life will get turned upside down. You don't know where or when it's coming, but it must be coming. Isn't that how the world works?

When life is good and you're still experiencing anxiety, sometimes the best thing you can do is just breathe and be mindful of the moment. Remind yourself of the great God you serve. Our God is a good, good Father. He loves His children. He wants you to live an abundant life full of blessing. Then allow the negative feelings to pass as you rest in God's faithful, loving arms.

He does not give and take away peace, as the world does. He just keeps giving out unending peace. Therefore, we don't need to let our hearts be troubled. We can trust in Him.

* * * * * * * * * * *

Dear God, thank You for Your everlasting peace.
I trust in You always, in good times and bad.

HE NEVER LEAVES

It is the LORD who goes before you. He will be with you;
he will not leave you or forsake you.
Do not fear or be dismayed.
DEUTERONOMY 31:8 ESV

One morning shortly after having my third child, I thought a trip to the mall would be a fun outing. My middle daughter, only three at the time, decided playing hide-and-seek in the mall would also be fun. Unfortunately, none of the rest of us knew we were playing a game! Thankfully, she was found quickly. But the terrifying memory of those few moments has not left me.

That fear of losing something we love, like the relationships we have with friends and loved ones, can cause anxiety. In contrast, how reassuring to know that the Lord has promised to never leave us or forsake us. Our ultimate friend, a companion who sticks closer than a brother, will never leave us alone. No matter where we wander or what circumstances we find ourselves in, He will never abandon us or give up on us. We need never fear or be dismayed because His promises are true and faithful. When life is more than we can bear, we can relax and rest in the assurance of His comforting presence!

Precious Lord, I praise You for Your faithful promise
to never leave or forsake me!

I WILL REFRESH
THE WEARY AND
SATISFY THE FAINT.

JEREMIAH 31:25 NIV

ESCAPE TO JESUS

You are my safe refuge, a fortress
where my enemies cannot reach me.

PSALM 61:3 NLT

Ever feel like you need a long, luxurious vacation? Like you need to rest in a cabin for a week or two, far from the demands of daily life?

Feelings of being overwhelmed can attack us, and life has a way of leaving us strung out, hankering for a mountain retreat or a beach vacation. When constant overload and stress strike, resist the temptation to tune out. Instead, tune in to Jesus.

We find relaxation at the feet of Jesus and can escape to Him every day. We don't need a cabin in the woods or a house on the beach to find the kind of soul rest we need. We don't even need a three-day weekend to find peace (but we wouldn't turn it down). Jesus offers a way to unwind in His presence right where we are.

Pour out your cares to the One who cares for you. Amid daily pressures, Jesus offers refuge. In stressful seasons, He is a safe refuge and fortress. Let His life bubble up in you today, washing away anxiety and stress. Say good-bye to overwhelm and hello to the rest only God can bring.

Jesus, teach me to escape to You,
not to things of the world.

FEEL GOD'S PRESENCE

If I go up to the heavens, you are there;
if I make my bed in the depths, you are there.
PSALM 139:8 NIV

Where are you right now? In your kitchen, perhaps, sitting at the table with a warm scone and cup of coffee. Or lying on your bed, perfectly relaxed, at peace. These are safe, familiar spaces, and you can probably feel it right now, if you try: the presence of God.

What about when you're in a different place? Like the hospital room where your mother lies ill? Or the conference room where you face the pressure to produce ideas or solutions? What about the courtroom where your son stands trial or the doctor's office where your diagnosis is delivered? Is the Spirit of God in those places too?

It's harder to believe so. Our experience of God is often shaped by our surroundings.

Yet here is a spectacular, amazing, comforting truth: There is no place where God is not. You cannot escape from His Spirit, even if you try. He is as present with you in your most tortured moments as in your most familiar surroundings. He will never leave you alone, and you can sense His presence right now, if you try. Breathe, and trust that He is with you.

* * * * * * * * * *

Lord, make Yourself known to me now, and later,
when I forget that You're here.

HEAVENLY LESSONS

The heavens are telling of the glory of God;
and their expanse is declaring the work of His hands.

PSALM 19:1 NASB

As a child growing up on a farm, one of the things my family did together was sit out on our front porch after supper in the summertime. One of my favorite things was counting "falling stars." Daddy pointed out the constellations and taught us their names.

To me this was a special time; I cherish those memories after all these years. As a child I enjoyed those quiet evenings, but now I realize my parents probably enjoyed them even more.

The time spent on the porch, after their work was done, was a time to release the pressures and busyness of the day. It was a time to breathe in the quietness and to let the beauty of the heavens surround them with peace.

Sometimes as an adult, whenever I gaze at the night sky, my mind goes back over the years, and I remember the lessons I learned on our front porch. Not only did I learn the names of the constellations, I learned to relax and enjoy those special times with my family.

✸ ✦ ✸ ✦ ✦ ✧ ✦ ✧ ✶ ✦ ✧

God of the heavens, remind me to let go of the busyness and learn to breathe in the peace of Your creation.

PASTORAL PEACE

Let the peace of Christ rule in your hearts.
COLOSSIANS 3:15 NASB

Have you ever visited a "pick-your-own" farm? Eager customers enter the garden, pick the fruits or vegetables they would like to purchase, and proudly take their harvest home.

What makes this chore appeal to people who could buy fresh produce elsewhere without physical labor? Maybe the allure is in pausing from daily chores, which provides an opportunity to take a deep breath and relax a bit. Or maybe glimpsing the countryside beauty of majestic trees, white fluffy clouds, and green pastures reminds us of God's power and creativity. Concerns seem to vanish in this setting.

When we're tired, frustrated, or fearful, inhaling outdoor air slowly produces calmness. Gazing up at a changeable blue sky often reminds us that the Creator of the earth is also our loving heavenly Father. This thought alone minimizes problems.

Nothing overwhelms Him. No challenge is too great for Him to solve. No concern is too small to mention in prayer. When we're fatigued, doubtful, or discouraged, a brief walk or drive to a rural area can inspire us to take a deep breath and enjoy peace as only He can give.

※ ※ ※ ※ ※ ※ ※ ※ ※ ※ ※

Lord Jesus, call me to rest my mind and body and to allow
Your peace to calm and govern my heart.

BECAUSE YOU LOVE ME, I CAN WAIT
WITH PERFECT PATIENCE
WELL POSSESSED;
BECAUSE YOU LOVE ME, ALL MY LIFE
IS CIRCLED WITH
UNQUESTIONED REST.

PAUL LAURENCE DUNBAR

A REST FOR THE SOUL

And you will find rest for your souls.

MATTHEW 11:29 NKJV

As the beach umbrella flapped gently in the wind, I soaked in the sounds around me. Seagulls squawking as they glided overhead. The crash of the waves as they broke onto the shore. My grandchildren laughing as they played in the water. The whisper of the ocean breezes as they wafted by.

Warm sunshine shone down on me, relaxing muscles that had been tight with tension when I arrived that day. When our family vacation finally began, I was weary. Physically. Emotionally. And, yes, even spiritually.

Long months of illness had taken their toll. My sixteenth surgical procedure had arrived unexpectedly in the form of an emergency that left me on bed rest for several weeks. I'd used up all my reserves. It felt like there was nothing left.

But as I sat on the sand that day with my family around me, I felt a sweet peace seep into my soul. I rested, soaking in the beauty of His creation, looking at the majesty and grandness of the ocean, and was reminded once again of the majesty and grandness of a God who can bring rest to our souls.

Father, thank You for sending moments that bring
sweet rest to my soul. Amen.

THIS MOMENT'S FREEDOM

The One who was born of God keeps them safe,
and the evil one cannot harm them.

1 JOHN 5:18 NIV

Is there such a place where we are truly safe? Thankfully, yes, and that place is right now. You're living in it. You're breathing, *reading*, and nothing is hurting you at this very moment. The world is turning, God is still on the throne, and you remain in the palm of His hand. You may have challenges, hardships, and strained relationships, but you're okay. Where you sit has your name engraved— from the beginning of time! What you are living out right now was assigned to you by God Himself.

Yesterday is done, and tomorrow has yet to come.

Being present is perfect—it's the only time that is completely known to us. We can relax, laugh, love, forgive, change, heal, offer and receive mercy, and hope. To live in the moment is to be truly free. Psalm 91:1 promises, "Those who live in the shelter of the Most High will find rest in the shadow of the Almighty" (NLT). *Abiding* is active and in the present tense. So abide, and find rest in the here and now.

* * * * * * * * * *

Father, teach me how to abide in each and every moment,
and to release to You my anxiety about
yesterday and tomorrow. Amen.

IT IS GOD WHO ARMS ME
WITH STRENGTH AND
KEEPS MY WAY SECURE.

2 SAMUEL 22:33 NIV

TRUSTING THAT HE USES US

Thanks be to God, who...uses us to spread the aroma
of the knowledge of him everywhere.

2 CORINTHIANS 2:14 NIV

Isn't it wonderful to know you lead a life of significance? Scripture says God uses us to spread the aroma of the knowledge of Him everywhere! It's easy to remember that in the big stuff, when we serve or give in an unusual way, but He's using us in the everyday stuff too.

Scripture often calls God good. When we live from His goodness, we share His lovely fragrance with the world! It's as simple as a kind comment on Facebook, a prayer breathed when we see a need, or being faithful in our work.

Cradling a precious child is sharing God's aroma with one He loves. When you rake someone's yard, plant a flower, or pick up trash, that's spreading His good scent. Living in integrity when it would be easier to cave in to dishonesty helps the world know His good, clean smell. The Bible says even when we offer someone a cup of cool water, we are doing His good work.

Relax. Embrace the wonder of this truth: your simple or significant life diffuses God's sweet smell throughout the world.

* * * * * * * * * *

Thank You, Lord, for inviting me into Your work
and for spreading Your sweet fragrance through me.

TAKE TIME TO UNWIND

Go, eat your food with gladness, and drink your wine
with a joyful heart, for God has already approved what you do.
ECCLESIASTES 9:7 NIV

I guess that's enough for now," I said, wiping my forehead. "I'll finish up in a minute." I'd been doing yard work all day but still had a few sticks to pick up.

"Are you kidding?" my friend asked. "It's after eight o'clock."

"But it stays light so long now. And there's so much to be done."

"It can wait," she said firmly. "There's only one Saturday this week, and you've missed most of it. Time to unwind."

Relaxation doesn't come naturally to achievement-oriented people like me—and perhaps you? Something in the back of the mind constantly prods us on. *You could be doing more. You haven't earned a rest. Now that the family is asleep, you should be getting some work done.*

Recognize that voice for what it is: your inner demon, trying to convince you that you must earn the love of others and that you never will.

God has accepted you. You don't need to earn His approval. In fact, you can't. So relax. Celebrate today and let tomorrow worry about itself.

* * * * * * * * * *

*Lord, teach me to feel the blessing of Your approval,
and to eat, drink, and be merry.*

IT'S QUIET IN HERE

He prepared the inner sanctuary within the temple
to set the ark of the covenant of the LORD there.

1 KINGS 6:19 NIV

It's a noisy world we live in—uneasy, impatient, and dissatisfied. Maybe it's always been that way, but to this extreme? Everyone's in a hurry, and no one seems to remember the subtle consideration of yesterday. Remember when we used to dole out grace by the cup full, offer a helping hand to a stranger, or make time to wait within our busy schedules? What's happened to us? Have we become numb to our animated surroundings, or perhaps deaf to the piercing sound of people's frustration?

Sweet is the silent stream that meanders through God's property—
that inner place where we can enter, day or night, to take cover in His still
serenity. A refuge where the walls are high and indestructible. A retreat
where no person, problem, or pain will find you. A spiritual Fort Knox of
impenetrable peace that lives within you, if only you will step inside and close
the door—tightly. Friend, relax, leave the turmoil outside, and safely shelter in
God's quiet place.

* * * * * * * * * * *

*My God, help me to find that inner peace amid the noise
of today. Help me to rest with calm assurance that I am safe
inside Your sanctuary. Amen.*

STRENGTH, REST,
GUIDANCE, GRACE, HELP,
SYMPATHY, LOVE—
ALL FROM GOD TO US!
WHAT A LIST OF BLESSINGS!

Evelyn Stenbock

SWEET SOUNDS

> For God so loved the world that He gave
> His only begotten Son, that whoever believes in Him
> should not perish but have everlasting life.
>
> JOHN 3:16 NKJV

For God so loved the world..." the angelic voice echoed through the auditorium.

My son's preschool teacher had taught the students Bible verses in the form of songs for their graduation ceremony, and she had assigned John 3:16 to my strong-willed child. Early in the process he decided he did not want to participate, so my wife and I prayed, coaxed, and eventually bribed him. "If you do your song, we'll get ice cream afterwards!"

He was stubborn, right up to the last minute. We held our breath as the teacher introduced him, and I was on the edge of my seat. "This is it, Lord," I prayed. "Help him."

Our little angel stepped up to the microphone and sang with no hesitation. A sweet peace washed over me—and the rest of the crowd—as he performed. He finished to thunderous applause, and my wife and I breathed a sigh of relief. God had proven Himself faithful, and we could relax. That post-ceremony ice cream tasted as good as any I've ever had.

Lord, help me to remember that You love my children
and I can trust You with them.

GOOD MORNING

Oh, taste and see that the LORD is good!
PSALM 34:8 ESV

It's morning—early. Your eyes open and *bang*! Your mind races into the day as if hijacked by a third party. First, it jolts you into unwilling participation. Next, your heart pounds as you ponder all of the uncertainties out of your control. It's a collection of anxiety from yesterday and future fears of tomorrow. And within seconds, you've handed over your happiness to stress and worry before putting your feet on the ground.

Wait! Start over.

It's morning—glorious morning. Whether there is sun, rain, kids, crazy job, it's a day the Lord has made. Say it out loud: "I WILL rejoice and be glad in it!" Take a deep breath, stay still for a minute just breathing in and out, in and out. Relax every muscle as you rest in God's peace and provision. This truly is a day He has made and given to you, and it's a gift that deserves a thank you. Before you do anything, dedicate the day to Him, thank Him, and look for Him in the *simplest things*.

My dear Father, thank You for going before me as I step out in faith, even into the current of everyday life.

ALL DAY LONG

I call to God, and the LORD saves me.
Evening, morning and noon I cry out in distress,
and he hears my voice.

PSALM 55:16–17 NIV

New parents wait with joyful anticipation for the first time their babies say "Mama" or "Dada." What delightful music those words are in the ears of a loving parent! The weary mother of multiple small children, however, may daydream about changing her name. "Mom, Mom, Mom…" All day long, her children call out to her for help with big and small tasks. What once was a joy can become tiresome to an overwhelmed parent. One mother of five once said that she was certain there was an alarm in the bathroom, ensuring that every time she withdrew for that necessary privacy a child would immediately cry out, "Mom?"

Our God does not grow tired like human parents. We can call upon Him evening, morning, and noon with the assurance He will not only hear us, but He will come to our aid. Like a loving parent, He anticipates our needs. God knows all about us and loves us anyway. He sees the solution to the problems that seem insurmountable to us. He will lift us up again, and again, and again.

Lord, thank You for never growing weary
of my cry for help. Amen.

COME UNTO ME, ALL YE THAT LABOUR AND ARE HEAVY LADEN, AND I WILL GIVE YOU REST.

MATTHEW 11:28 KJV

PERFECT PEACE

You will keep in perfect peace those whose minds
are steadfast, because they trust in you.

ISAIAH 26:3 NIV

The little kangaroo in its mother's pouch provides a lesson in trust. Flying through the outback, the mother runs up to 40 miles per hour. In God's ingenious design, the opening of the pouch faces upward, preventing the baby from falling out even at high speeds. The cozy pocket keeps the joey secure as he goes along for the ride, providing a warm, safe place for him to grow up. Imagine the bouncing, the jolting, the jarring of a ride in a kangaroo pouch. Anchored firmly, the baby kangaroo remains tucked away, intuitively understanding steadfast trust. And when he is ready, he emerges, unscathed, ready to bounce on his own.

Human beings could learn from this tiny creature of the Australian outback. We need firm mooring, a place of security and safety amidst the bumps and jolts of life. God has designed for us a way to find that shelter. When we trust God, fixing our minds upon Him, we are promised perfect peace. Like a little joey in its mother's pouch, we are carried by One much stronger and wiser than us, and our minds are guarded with God's perfect peace.

Lord, help me choose to fix my mind on You,
trusting You steadfastly today. Amen.

A HELPER ON MY SIDE

The LORD is on my side as my helper.
PSALM 118:7 ESV

The kitchen was covered in flour. Sugar sprinkled the floor, and eggshells were scattered across the countertop. The little girl was cooking with her mother, and from the looks of it, things were a mess. Until one listened. Laughter rose up as the dry ingredients made a cloud, and giggles punctuated the air as the sticky mess transformed to cookie dough. The mother's quiet voice could be heard here and there explaining how to measure, what a whisk is, why baking powder is necessary.

An hour later, the young chef and her helper sat at the table with mugs of creamy milk and a plateful of warm cookies, enjoying what they had accomplished together.

Our projects can often look like a flour-covered, sugar-sprinkled mess. We need a wise helper to laugh with us, instruct us, and see us through to the rewarding end. God is at our side as our Helper, and He rejoices in the task. The mess doesn't matter. It just means we are learning with God. If your mess is troubling you today, remember your Helper. He is at your side, and He delights in you as you work together.

* * * * * * * * * *

Lord, please come alongside me in my mess,
and help me make something wonderful. Amen.

RESTING IN OUR REFUGE

The LORD is good, a refuge in times of trouble.
He cares for those who trust in him.
NAHUM 1:7 NIV

He loves you, you know. He sees you. When you laugh and your heart is full. And in those awful times when it hurts so much you go numb.

He enjoys the happy days with you. He loves it when you dance in joy, and sends the sweetness of His presence to increase your mutual delight. He also understands your fight to trust Him on the bad days, and He comes whispering love and peace. "Remember My goodness," He says. "I'm dedicated to meeting you right there in the middle of the trouble."

He's not far away. In fact, He's as close as your very breath.

Do you sense His whisper? "Make Me your refuge," He says. "I am your strong tower. I am the rock where you stand steady. I shelter you beneath My wings. Even as a nursing momma never forgets her baby, I can never forget you. I stand like a momma bear over you. I am here. Always."

Take a deep breath. Let His love penetrate the chaos. Let Him still the storm within your heart. He is good. He will never abandon you. He cares about everything you care about.

* * * * * * * * * *

You are my refuge, Lord, and I trust You.

53

IN THOSE TIMES
I CAN'T SEEM TO FIND GOD,
I REST IN THE ASSURANCE
HE KNOWS HOW TO FIND ME.

NEVA COYLE

HOPE FOR THE FUTURE

"I know the plans I have for you," says the LORD.
"They are plans for good and not for disaster,
to give you a future and a hope."

JEREMIAH 29:11 NLT

When the world presses in and our lives seem to be in total chaos, remembering God's love can be difficult. The more stressed and fearful we become, the more the temptation to seek answers in other places can feel like a craving hunger. We want help and answers.

But no one knows us the way God does. He has known us—and His plans for us—from the time of our conception (Jeremiah 1:5). Even when we don't know our own minds, He does. His designs for us are never *against* us. He sees "the big picture," and His love and mercy will bring good in our lives, no matter how rough the journey is at this moment. He wants peace for us, and hope for our future.

God does not forget about us, and His mercy and kindness continually surround us, even when it feels like life is completely out of control. When we remember that, when we rely on that, we can find that a calm peace will settle on us.

Lord, when life delivers chaos into my life, help me remember that You only desire good for me. When I trust in You, I can have hope for my future. Amen.

FILLED WITH PEACE

You, O LORD, are a shield around me; you are my glory,
the one who holds my head high.

PSALM 3:3 NLT

When we feel overwhelmed, when it seems life is on the offensive and we're assailed by the fiery darts of the enemy: the Lord is our shield. He surrounds us with His presence. There are no chinks in this protection. He will not allow anything to harm us not meant for our ultimate good. We need not fear any attack.

When we feel worried over what others think, when we feel our reputation is under scrutiny or our good name is wrongly maligned: the Lord is our glory.

We don't need to strive to make everyone happy. We have nothing to prove. His glory is complete and sufficient; we need only to trust and obey.

When we feel discouraged, downtrodden, as if we're carrying the weight of our world on our shoulders: the Lord is the lifter of our head. He reaches out to us, gently invites us to lift our eyes up from our difficult circumstances and look full in His wonderful face. We need not let our circumstances have the final say, but instead we can meet His loving gaze and be filled with peace.

* * * * * * * * * *

Tender Father, make us sensitive to Your presence.
Fill us with confidence in Your protection, and replace
our anxiety with Your perfect peace.

THE ART OF GIVING UP

The LORD himself will fight for you. Just stay calm.
EXODUS 14:14 NLT

I watch him try and shove his foot into the shoe, growing more frustrated each second. I could step in, but I choose to wait. I know I can't teach my son anything until he's ready to learn.

Finally, I hear those magic words: "Mom, can you help?"

In similar fashion, God often waits for us to ask Him, to demonstrate our reliance on Him. He longs for us to depend on Him and give up trying to live life on our own. After all, God gives His grace to the weak ones who ask, not the religious strength trainers.

This isn't giving up in defeat, but surrendering to God as the Israelites learned to do in the wilderness. God wants to fight for us, but first we need to be still. God longs to help us in every situation, if we'll only wait and rest in Him. So often we muddle through each day on our own when infinite grace awaits us.

Waiting on God is difficult, but it's much easier than plowing through our days without God's grace.

* * * * * * * * * *

Father, I surrender to You today; as I rest and wait on You,
please pour Your grace over my life.

ENJOY THE QUIET

All the lands are at rest and at peace; they break into singing.

ISAIAH 14:7 NIV

After every storm in life, a kind of calm descends. This happens in the most mundane ways, like when you experience that deafening calm after the baby goes to sleep. This vacuum occurs at more poignant moments too, like when the house becomes eerily quiet after the last teenager moves out. Whatever the tsunami—an illness, a heartbreak, a job loss—it will be followed by a calm, an emptiness, a dead space.

Our temptation is to fill in that space with more activity. We go looking for something—noise, commotion, relationships, anything to fill the void.

We volunteer for one more job at church or get coffee with one more acquaintance or take on more hours at work or start some new venture.

Don't. Be still for just a moment. Enjoy this quiet while it lasts.

There's nothing wrong with this space. It's not empty; it's filled with silence. It's not wasted; it's restful. Soon enough you can add back all those good activities—if you still want to.

For now, put on another pot of tea, go to your favorite chair, and just enjoy the quiet. This, too, is a gift from God.

* * * * * * * * * * *

Lord, lead me to rest before the next storm comes.

CAST YOUR CARES
ON THE LORD AND
HE WILL SUSTAIN YOU.

PSALM 55:22 NIV

GOD NEVER CHANGES

The LORD directs the steps of the godly.
He delights in every detail of their lives.
PSALM 37:23-24 NLT

As we drove away, leaving our eighteen-year-old daughter in downtown Los Angeles to begin her freshman year of fashion school, I tried hard to hold back the tears but I was unsuccessful. I thought I was prepared for that moment, but when it actually happened, it was obvious I wasn't. I didn't want to "embrace change" like all the parenting books about empty-nesting had instructed. I just wanted things to go back to the way they were, with both of my daughters at home, piled on my bed, watching chick flicks with me.

Change, whether we're ready for it or not, can be a little scary. It can leave us feeling vulnerable, anxious, and fearful. I was all three that day we left our baby girl in LA, but as I dug into God's Word, I was reminded that He never changes. He is our stability, our comforter, and our protector. We don't have to worry about the future because God has already been there, and He will go with us every step of the way.

* * * * * * * * * * *

Father, help me to trust You more, and help me to face my future with hope, not dread. Amen.

PAUSE FOR A TIME-IN

I have calmed and quieted myself...
like a weaned child I am content.

PSALM 131:2 NIV

Ever been sent to time-out? As the beloved of Christ, we can enjoy time-*in*. Time-outs put us on the couch, in the corner, or at the back of the classroom, but time-ins can happen *anywhere*. In the shower. On the freeway. When we wait for a doctor's appointment. Even in a room full of people.

Time-ins can last thirty seconds or two hours. We can enjoy a time-in many times every day.

A time-in is simply a pause to embrace complete dependence on Jesus and all He does for us. It's a moment to remember you're *all in* with Him, and He's *all in* with you. We let go of faults because they're already forgiven. We cease striving. After all, He planted the Holy Spirit within us, and He's empowering us to do good. When we take a time-in, we remember that.

Time-ins refocus swirling thoughts to trust. Time-ins replace guilt and striving with peace. Time-ins receive and offer love. Time-ins invite quiet strength as we reflect on God and our complete dependence on Him.

* * * * * * * * * *

Here I am, Jesus, taking a time-in and remembering
all You've done for me.

TRUSTING THE NAME OF GOD

Those who know your name trust in you, for you, LORD,
have never forsaken those who seek you.

PSALM 9:10 NIV

There are times in every believer's life when he or she feels like God is very far away. Those times may come when we have sinned, suffered a tremendous setback in life, lost a loved one, or let quiet time with God slip by the wayside.

Have you ever felt that way? Where you know you should probably read your Bible or go to church, but you just don't feel like it. All you can do is sit.

What is the one thing that remains constant during those times?

What is the only thing you can cling to? The name of the Lord. Often all you can do is whisper His name. Say it over and over. You know the power that is there but you are not able to get beyond the mere utterance of that Name.

But with each murmur of His name, you bring yourself closer to reconnecting with Him and feeling the power that is within you because you are His.

Do you need refreshment today? Just sit quietly and breathe the name of Jesus.

Lord, thank You that grasping hold of Your power in my life is as simple as speaking Your name. Amen.

AS THE CHAOS SWIRLS
AND LIFE'S DEMANDS
PULL AT ME ON ALL SIDES,
I WILL BREATHE IN
GOD'S PEACE.

ANONYMOUS

MY QUIET PLACE

Jesus often withdrew to lonely places and prayed.

LUKE 5:16 NIV

When my son and I moved, we left our home, church, friends, and everything familiar. I underestimated the impact of giving up my home office, which had been my work area and my place to meet with God. We'd moved in with my parents, so privacy was almost impossible to find. I longed for a special spot for prayer, reflection, or to pray over the phone with a friend without anyone overhearing.

I found the perfect haven while taking a walk—a bench that was just secluded enough to feel like a secret getaway. That became my place to escape to when I needed a moment alone with God to cry out to or thank Him, to rest my mind after a stressful day, or to connect with a prayer partner. Every walk that includes a stop at the bench—even for only a moment—calms me in a unique way.

Jesus needed "lonely places" to meet with His heavenly Father, and so do we. They can be hard to find, but when we find one, it becomes sacred. Where is your quiet place? When is the last time you spent a few precious minutes there?

* * * * * * * * * *

Lord, provide the private moments
that I need with You today.

THE QUEEN OF CHAOS

God is not the author of confusion, but of peace.

1 Corinthians 14:33 KJV

I don't like mess or chaos. That's ironic since my life is filled with those things. Some days my to-do list is so long that I'm sure it must stretch to Kansas. And I've found it doesn't help when I add a major remodeling project to the mix, one that somehow ends up in every room with saws grinding, hammers pounding, and workmen coming in and out. And then there's the sheetrock dust, ladders, boards, buckets, and tools all over the house. Yes folks, total chaos.

But then I realized something that helped me. I cleaned one room that wasn't having much work done in it, a room that was somewhat away from the mayhem. When I needed to write or when the chaos in the rest of the house started driving me crazy, I could go to that quiet, restful place and feel an instant peace.

The same is true spiritually. When life starts getting me down, when the chaos of my to-do list starts overwhelming me, I can go to my quiet place, to the God who is the author of peace, and I can find rest for my soul.

* * * * * * * * *

Father, remind me that true rest
is found in You. Amen.

A WEEK OF PRIMITIVE LIVING

Then, because so many people were coming
and going that they did not even have a chance to eat,
he said to them, "Come with me by yourselves
to a quiet place and get some rest."

MARK 6:31 NIV

While my son looked forward to summer camp, I anticipated a week at a friend's cabin. After an exhausting year, time with two sisters in Christ felt like the perfect respite.

"Just as a heads up," Anne warned me, "Rebecca's cabin doesn't have Internet access or cell service. There's a landline for urgent calls."

For once I didn't mind! Usually I would take my laptop to work on a writing project. I left it at home. If I wrote, it would be in my journal with a pen. I expected to go through withdrawals. I didn't. Instead of spending the week fighting the pull of a screen, my friends and I took walks, sat on the deck, and enjoyed long talks and fits of laughter. We only turned on the TV to watch old movies at night. I went home rejuvenated.

Jesus knew when His disciples needed rest, and He knows when our best refreshment will come from trading technology for time with people and enjoying His creation.

Lord, provide a place to rest when my soul is tired.

LET MY HEART,
THIS SEA OF RESTLESS WAVES,
FIND PEACE IN YOU, O GOD.

AUGUSTINE

PARADIGM SHIFT

So it is written: "The first man Adam became a living being";
the last Adam, a life-giving spirit.

1 CORINTHIANS 15:45 NIV

The pressures of some days take our breath away. It's hard to keep all the balls in the air. We don't want to let anyone down.

In times like this it's easy to wonder where the abundant life God promised is found. Our thoughts are about survival; it's like we forget to breathe. But in the beginning the Father gave us the breath of life; after the cross, Jesus gave us the life-giving Spirit. Surely He didn't intend for us to constantly be off and running, gasping for air. Perhaps He whispers, "Stop. Linger. Breathe Me."

Maybe our paradigm needs a shift. Maybe it's not about doing everything for God or for those whom He's put in our lives. Maybe instead of being about the doing, it is really about the receiving of Him. Pausing. Trusting. Allowing Him to infuse us with all that is needed to face each day, even the really crazy ones. What if breathing is not simply a physical act of taking in air to stay alive, but also a spiritual act of taking in the breath of empowering grace?

* * * * * * * * * * *

Help me to breathe in and out today by Your Spirit, Jesus, receiving Your empowering grace.

GOD, MY SOURCE

Don't worry about anything; instead, pray about everything.
Tell God what you need, and thank him for all he has done.

PHILIPPIANS 4:6 NLT

The unthinkable had happened. My children and I were on our own as a result of divorce. My small salary seldom stretched from payday to payday, and inventive manipulation of the budget had to be enacted. I learned to cut corners, reuse, do without, and hang on to God's promise that He would provide. And He did. Over and over, again and again.

Extra things such as tires, car repairs, shoes, and anything out of the ordinary caused me to rethink my budget. I learned valuable lessons during that time. One of the lessons learned was dependency on an awesome God. He was always ready to hold us close to Him and provide what we needed.

Whenever discouragement threatened and I was on the verge of giving up, I paused and gave thanks to God for what He had given us and for the closeness and love we shared. At those times I breathed in the peace that passes understanding and breathed out negative thoughts and attitudes. He assured me that He is my source and reminded me how faithful He is.

God of provision, remind us always that You alone
are our source. You are faithful.

PEACE BEYOND STRESS

The LORD blesses his people with peace.

PSALM 29:11 NIV

I used to have a narrow view of the word peace. It always brought to mind calm settings, perfectly clean houses, and relationships without conflict. For me, peace was a bubble that burst anytime my stress level increased.

It's hard to live like that. It leads to all kinds of false expectations, especially in light of how many times God promises us peace. So I began to dig in and search out what it means to have God's peace.

I discovered it's more powerful than anything I imagined, and it goes beyond just the absence of stress. It comes when I focus on God, instead of my situation.

I found that when I draw closer to God, He gives me peace that flows through any circumstances I'm facing. For me, God's peace is the certainty that He's in control and that no matter the difficulties, something better lies ahead.

* * * * * * * * * * *

Dear Lord, don't ever let me try to live without
Your peace flowing through my life. Amen.

WORN-OUT BAGGAGE

The LORD will work out his plans for my life—
for your faithful love, O LORD, endures forever.
PSALM 138:8 NLT

I was beyond overwhelmed. There was no other way to describe it—and the bad part was that I had no control over any of my stressful situations. I knew that, but since I'm sometimes a slow learner, I still tried to fix things myself.

Numerous responsibilities, issues with our family business, serious health problems, and multiple tight deadlines had left me so burdened that I didn't feel like I could make it through another day. Finally (remember the slow learner?) I got down on my knees and said, "God, I can't deal with these situations. I'm going to leave them with You and let You handle them."

Sounds great, huh? It would have been except there was one slight problem. The next morning, I picked up that baggage again—worrying, stressing, and trying to help God fix things. I wish I could say that was a one-time occurrence, but I've worn that baggage out over the years. Can any of you relate?

I'm so grateful God is patient with us and that He can handle our burdens without any problem—especially when we don't try to help Him.

* * * * * * * * * *

Lord, help me to bring my burdens to You—
and to leave them there. Amen.

BE STILL,
AND KNOW THAT
I AM GOD.

PSALM 46:10 ESV

TIME FOR A BEAUTY BREAK

How many are your works, LORD! In wisdom
you made them all; the earth is full of your creatures.

PSALM 104:24 NIV

We hurry, worry, and try to somehow hold it all together. The chaos of modern life leaves us fazed, and daily stress can shrivel our souls.

A simple remedy exists with the power to refresh us at our core. We can take a beauty break—a pause to relish God.

Beauty hints of another world, the world of order and peace where God, our intelligent designer, dwells. Beauty awakens our hearts to worship and connects us to the One who makes all things beautiful in His time.

Step outside for fifteen minutes to drink in creation's glory. You might see a butterfly take flight or let the sunset steal your breath away. Sidestep your desk or that sink full of dishes to exhale and remember how our Father plants beauty everywhere.

Psalm 104 revels in creation's beauty and reminds us to praise its Maker. It concludes with these words: "I will sing to the Lord all my life; I will sing praise to my God as long as I live" (verse 33 NIV).

Short beauty breaks train our minds to behold and bask in God's presence. Let beauty become the maestro of your heart, leading you to nonstop adoration.

Father, teach me to pause throughout the day
to glimpse Your beauty.

ELIJAH AND THE THIN QUIET

> After the fire, there was a sound. Thin. Quiet.
>
> 1 KINGS 19:12 CEB

One of the holiest moments I've ever experienced was in my college dorm room during a thunderstorm with two friends. We painted, sang songs, celebrated Communion with Twinkies and Coke, and eventually the electricity went out. Silence.

Sometimes I expect to encounter God's presence in grandiose ways, but more often than not, it's simpler than that.

God told Elijah to stand at the base of a mountain for God to pass by.

A strong wind tore through the mountains. Elijah searched for God in the wind, but no luck. After the wind came an earthquake, but God wasn't there. Then came a fire, burning trees and the ground around him. God wasn't there either. But after the fire, there was calm. The Hebrew word is sometimes translated as "Thin. Quiet."

God shows up unexpectedly in the simplicity of our lives—in the mundane, unspectacular, and routine. When we recognize God in the thin quiet, life becomes sacramental. Your experiences, relationships, struggles, and joys are drenched in the divine. The secular becomes sacred, the mundane becomes holy, and the boring becomes beautiful.

* * * * * * * * * *

God of the thin quiet, pass by me today even
in the seemingly mundane parts. Help me to remember
that You are with me always.

GOD KNOWS THE RHYTHM
OF MY SPIRIT AND KNOWS
MY HEART THOUGHTS.
HE IS AS CLOSE AS BREATHING.

ANONYMOUS

JESUS LOVED MARTHA

Now Jesus loved Martha, and her sister, and Lazarus.

JOHN 11:5 KJV

When my Martha takes over and my Mary goes to hide, when my busyness overcomes my desire to sit at His feet, when I am overwhelmed with to-do lists and deadlines instead of resting in His presence, what comfort there is to remember that Jesus loved Martha too. Yes, there are better choices. Yes, I am troubled about many things instead of the most important thing. But Jesus still loves me. He made me. He knows me. And even in my frenzy and bustle and distraction, He never stops loving me.

In John 11, when Martha and Mary sent for Jesus since Lazarus was deathly ill, the Healer waited. He didn't respond immediately. But it wasn't because He didn't love them. He had bigger plans—astounding, miraculous plans! His delay provided their opportunity to be eyewitnesses to His power as He raised Lazarus from the grave. When you call for His help, and you think His response is slow, don't mistake it for a lack of love. Even when we don't understand God's work or His timing, we can rest in the confidence that He loves us.

Jesus, You loved Martha,
and I am so thankful that You love me too.

RETRAINING YOUR MIND

Cast all your anxiety on him because he cares for you.

1 PETER 5:7 NIV

Like muddy paw prints on a newly waxed floor, the cares of life can prance into our well-ordered world unwelcomed. Hopeful mornings become clogged inside of us. Worries build to pressure cooker temperature as we fret.

Fussing over problems feels natural. Required. But anxious thoughts don't solve anything. In them we find no helpful perspective. No comforting reassurance. Anxiety only confirms we are stressed—which we already knew!

The psalmist poured his complaints before the same God who welcomes us to give Him our struggles. But like the poet-king, we don't stop with the grumbling. Instead we pause and trust our good God. He's proven faithful time and again, handling the messy parts of life. We step into peace as He invites us to release problems and anxiety into His capable care. He loves us and is pleased to help.

Sometimes He solves everything in a snap; usually He invites us to grab hold of His strong hand, walk a little slower, and just breathe. He sees the bigger perspective and works for good. As His plan unfolds He is with us. His loving care comforts. His wisdom guides. His confidence reassures. His strength uplifts.

* * * * * * * * * *

Dear Jesus, thank You for taking my anxiety
and replacing it with peace.

A LIFE TRANSFORMED
BY THE POWER OF GOD
IS ALWAYS A MARVEL
AND A MIRACLE.

GERALDINE NICHOLAS

THE CHOREOGRAPHER

We do not know what to do, but our eyes are upon you.

2 CHRONICLES 20:12 NIV

The little prima ballerina hopefuls lined up like teetering dolls on the stage. Under the bright lights their costumes twinkled and sparkled as every child squinted to focus on the teacher, who was discreetly hiding in the shadows. They had practiced the routine for months and today was the big day. Step, by twirl, by plié, each little one persevered through Schubert's *Rosamunde* to the beautiful end. The audience rose to their feet with roaring applause.

Sometimes life seems to be a choreographed dance that we have tried hard to master but fear to fail. So many eyes are on us, watching every step. If we focus on our audience, we may lose courage and stumble. But when we peer into the face of God, the choreographer of our lives, we are steadied and strengthened. His face is all the certainty we need.

When we just don't know what to do, or how we will make it through, we can look to God and trust Him to guide us. We are not alone. He may seem hidden in the shadows, but He is there, watching, coaching, helping us as we focus on Him.

* * * * * * * * * *

Lord, help me to fix my eyes on You
and press on to the end. Amen.

DEEP BREATHS

So we fix our eyes not on what is seen, but on what is unseen,
since what is seen is temporary, but what is unseen is eternal.

2 CORINTHIANS 4:18 NIV

When anxiety strikes, a common remedy is to count to ten, letting deep breaths in and out of our lungs. As we do, we stop dwelling on the problem at hand and focus on something more fundamental: air.

Similarly, we can adjust our lens to see God's plan when we're overwhelmed. To do this, we stand on our tiptoes to look beyond short-term circumstances or conflicts.

Looking back, we see that God is the One who breathed life into us.

Scripture says, "Your eyes saw my unformed body; all the days ordained for me were written in your book before one of them came to be" (Psalm 139:16 NIV).

Looking forward, we know that God has cleared a path to our heavenly home. For those who follow Christ, our way is already paid: "For no one can lay any foundation other than the one already laid, which is Jesus Christ" (1 Corinthians 3:11 NIV).

God's plan is fundamental, our foundation. Like a breath of fresh air, set your sights on heaven today, looking beyond the temporary obstacles.

Father, when I face a trial, help me to see
Your bigger purpose for my life.

THE ANSWER TO MY FEAR

I sought the LORD, and he answered me
and delivered me from all my fears.

PSALM 34:4 ESV

I'm a person who craves order. No matter the circumstance, I want to know what's coming so I can have a plan in place. Yep, you guessed it, I'm a card-carrying control freak. This is never more evident than when I'm afraid. In the past, my way of coping with fear was to look for answers—remedies—to alleviate my fears. I'd worry over every detail of what might happen, mapping out scenarios and ways to cope. It was exhausting to me—and to those around me.

One morning, I read this verse and it seemed to leap off the page at me.

Could it be this simple? Hesitantly, I began to pray. I asked God to take my fear and replace it with His peace. He immediately answered me, enveloping me in His presence and His peace. The circumstances hadn't changed, but I had.

In turning to Him, I acknowledged that even if I don't have all the answers, God does. And He's big enough, wise enough, and loving enough to carry me through any scenario.

❋ ❋ ❋ ❋ ❋ ❋ ❋ ❋ ❋ ❋

Dear Lord, help me to always turn to You first
when I'm afraid and looking for answers. Amen.

MAY THE GOD OF
LOVE AND PEACE
SET YOUR HEART
AT REST.

RAYMOND OF PENYAFORT

LET JESUS MOVE YOUR MOUNTAIN

"Not by might nor by power, but by my Spirit,"
says the LORD Almighty.
ZECHARIAH 4:6 NIV

Close your eyes and look at your mountain—that very large thing that's keeping you from moving forward. Is it fear or anger? Maybe a health issue or personal dilemma. Whatever it is, it's big! And after doing everything in your power to change it, sweet talk it, beat it senseless, or ignore it, you end up exhausted and suddenly aware that it's simply too mammoth for you to lift.

Girl, don't you know that anything God has put your name on never requires force? He is the Lord of the meek; the Prince of Peace; the One who said, "Be still, and know I am God!" In our fiercest efforts to move things around, we take the responsibility away from the One who allowed them there in the first place. What God requires from us is to hand over everything to Him…*everything*. It's grace that we don't have to fight for what belongs to us. Jesus will handle it, so just sit back and let your Man do the heavy lifting!

My dear God, in all of my crazy effort,
I somehow forgot that You are in control.
Remind me that I don't have to be strong
when it's Jesus moving the mountains. Amen.

POURING OUT A WATERFALL

Trust in him at all times, O people; pour out your heart
before him; God is a refuge for us.

PSALM 62:8 ESV

We took our kids on a cross-country road trip this past spring, trekking from the West Coast to the East Coast, and back again. One of our last stops was spent exploring Yellowstone National Park. Besides the otherworldly geothermal pools, a favorite stop was the vista above the Upper Falls of the Yellowstone River. The enormous waterfall cascades 109 feet, crashing into the gorge of Yellowstone's Grand Canyon.

This is the picture that comes to mind when I consider pouring out my heart to the Lord. When I am desperately seeking refuge, when life is full of churning whitewater, I need to know I have a Father who can handle the raging deluge.

Not only is He able to receive all we pour out, He transforms our splashing chaos into beauty.

Sometimes He does this by slowing the rush to a calm stream, like the glassy tributaries that meander across Yellowstone's grassy meadows. Other times He strengthens our banks, enabling us to sustain the surge, giving others a chance to bask breathless in the beauty and wonder of a person surrendered to His will.

❋ ❋ ❋ ❋ ❋ ❋ ❋ ❋ ❋

Father, I pour out the rushing waters of my heart to You.
Give peace, strength, and redeeming beauty.

RESTING IN WORSHIP

He said: "Listen, King Jehoshaphat and all who live in Judah
and Jerusalem! This is what the LORD says to you:
'Do not be afraid or discouraged because of this vast army.
For the battle is not yours, but God's.'"

2 CHRONICLES 20:15 NIV

One night when my youngest daughter was an infant, nothing I did soothed her. Food, clean diaper, favorite toy, mommy snuggles—nothing worked. Finally I dimmed the lights in the bedroom, turned on my worship playlist, and held her as I sang and swayed my way around the room. And suddenly in the darkness, God was there. She wailed. I worshipped.

Sometimes in stressful situations the best thing we can do is worship. Worship refocuses our hearts on God's power and reminds us that the battle belongs to Him. That's what happened for King Jehoshaphat. After a prophet reminded him that the battle belonged to the Lord, Jehoshaphat had the army march out to battle singing. As they rested in worship and the knowledge of who God was, God won the victory for them.

We too can rest in the power of worship. When conflict comes, rest in your knowledge of who God is. Dedicate your heart to worship. Then let God bring you the victory.

Lord, in times of conflict and stress
I will rest in worshiping You.

IN QUIETNESS AND CONFIDENCE SHALL BE YOUR STRENGTH.

Isaiah 30:15 NKJV

PRESENT TROUBLES

Our present troubles are small and won't last very long.
Yet they produce for us a glory that vastly
outweighs them and will last forever!
2 CORINTHIANS 4:17 NLT

In California's Sonoma Valley, grape fields stretch wide across rich soil. This viticulture hot spot draws wine enthusiasts worldwide. They come to taste the rich flavor and variety of wines in the area, but few know the duress the grapes undergo.

Stressed grapes produce the best wine, so winemakers often stress the vines on purpose to enhance flavor. For instance, if grapes have too much water, they become flaccid and the flavor is weak. So, growers impose drought to rid the fruit of excess water and bring out the flavor of the fruit.

In a similar way, God, our divine Vinedresser, allows the pressures of this life to bring out the best flavor in us.

We won't escape hard times, but we can rest knowing that our present trouble is only temporary. God knows exactly what He's doing in our lives. He knows our end from our beginning. The Author and Finisher of our faith has plans to bring a rich flavor out of the trials of our lives, producing in us eternal glory.

All the problems swirling around us just cannot compare to our glorious future.

Lord Jesus, teach me to rest in my stress today, knowing that
You have a plan, one that extends into eternity.

GOD'S SAFE HOUSE

The LORD is a shelter for the oppressed,
a refuge in times of trouble.

PSALM 9:9 NLT

Where was your safe place when you were a child? I had a treehouse with walls and a sturdy ladder—high up above everyone else. There I could escape the noise, conflict, or the crowd. I could dream. I felt comfortable, cozy, and somehow protected.

Perhaps you had a bedroom corner, a homemade tent, or a spot in the backyard. But where do you go today, now that you're a grown-up and it seems impossible to hide from the world? Even if you have a favorite easy chair, reality encroaches as cell phones beckon and people demand that you meet their immediate needs.

But who will meet *your* need for security and safety? Where can you still the pounding of your heart, breathe calmly, and know deep in your soul that you are truly loved and accepted?

Only in the Lord. As the psalmist says, He alone is our shelter when we are oppressed. God alone is our "refuge in times of trouble."

He is the best safe house ever! Because no matter where we are or what is happening, we can rest in His protective presence.

*Lord, the world is scary; help me turn to You
for continual refuge. Amen.*

BREATHE IN GRACE

Out of his fullness we have all received grace
in place of grace already given.

JOHN 1:16 NIV

Perfectionism is a joy-stealer, especially when it's a lifestyle. But you don't have to be a perfectionist to feel like a failure. Feelings of failure can blindside us. It can be as simple as forgetting to return a call or set an alarm or burning dinner. It can be as complicated as struggling in relationship with someone important to us.

God never thinks of us as failures. When He looks at us, He sees the success of Jesus. That doesn't mean we never mess up; it means His grace is right there waiting for us when we do. Not only did God already give us that wonderful, covering grace that fills us with Christ's righteousness, but He also offers empowering grace so we can forgive ourselves and move forward. When we need to respond to our place of struggle and rectify the situation, He gives more grace! Through His Spirit He guides us, showing us how to handle difficult circumstances, and then He carries us through the experience by His grace. It's *all* Him! Hallelujah!

Pause. Breathe in the grace.

It's always there. Given freely. Embrace it.

❋ ❋ ❋ ❋ ❋ ❋ ❋ ❋ ❋

Father, when I'm tempted to berate myself, please help me pause, accept the grace already mine, and move forward.

HE ALWAYS PROVIDES

Don't worry about these things, saying, "What will we eat?
What will we drink? What will we wear?" These things dominate
the thoughts of unbelievers, but your heavenly Father already
knows all your needs. Seek the Kingdom of God above all else,
and live righteously, and he will give you everything you need.

MATTHEW 6:31–33 NLT

It had been weeks and still no word on a job for my dear husband. Our savings had begun to dwindle to nothing and the prospect of how we would pay our bills was looming over our heads. We were uncertain of how this would all come together and trust was our only option.

Day after day we prayed. Each day money would show up in one form or another; a rebate from a forgotten purchase or refunds from places we did not know owed us. It covered all of our needs.

Trusting God in times of need had never been a strong suit for me, yet this time was different. When I was brought to the edge I chose to step out in faith, and His response was "I will give you what you need."

* * * * * * * * * *

Father God, when the worries of how and when overcome me,
calm my soul with Your promise that You will provide
all my needs. Strengthen my trust in You.

IN CHRIST, WE ARE RELAXED
AND AT PEACE IN THE MIDST
OF THE CONFUSIONS...
AND PERPLEXITIES
OF THIS LIFE.

BILLY GRAHAM

MORE THAN AN OVERCOMER

I can do all things through Christ
who strengthens me.
PHILIPPIANS 4:13 NKJV

When we hear the word "Nike," we tend to think of shoes or athletic wear. To the Greeks, Nike is the Greek goddess of victory. Did you know "Nike" has a biblical connection? Revelation 3:21 states, "…to him who overcomes…." The phrasing comes from the Greek word *nikao*. Athletes are called upon to be victorious, or overcomers, in their careers. In life, God calls us to do the same. As my pastor recently shared, God wants us to be a *hupernikao*, which means "more than an overcomer."

The blood of Jesus has made us overcomers, or *hupernikaos*. Through Jesus, there is nothing we cannot achieve. This knowledge is powerful, as it allows us to gain victory over any stress that comes our way.

Even in challenging situations, it is possible to let go and trust that God has a good outcome in mind. It takes time to overcome patterns of worry, anxiety, and fear, but you are not left alone to do battle. If you are going to doubt something, doubt your doubts and fears.

Lord, through Your power, I can stay
in the fight and overcome every situation
placed before me today. Amen.

GOD'S WISDOM

If any of you lacks wisdom, let him ask of God,
who gives to all generously and without reproach,
and it will be given to him.

JAMES 1:5 NASB

It was a difficult time. Every alternative to the situation facing me—including not moving at all—would make things worse. I needed help. I turned to a friend of mine for wisdom, and she pointed me to this verse. I told her that I'd read it and asked for wisdom, but God was silent.

"God is silent because He's already answered."

I stared at her. "That's what I mean. I don't hear His answer."

"You don't have to hear His answer for it to be there." She smiled. "God is always true to His Word. When we ask for wisdom, He provides it. The next step is ours to take."

She just wasn't getting it. "But I don't know which step to take."

Again that Mona Lisa smile. "Take a step and you'll see. God has given you all you need."

Could it be this simple?

I was desperate so I took the step. Sure enough, it was the exact right step. I began applying this verse to more and more situations. God has never failed me.

* * * * * * * * * *

Dear Lord, help me step in faith
when I'm struggling. Amen.

NEVER ALONE

Of Benjamin he said, "The beloved of the LORD dwells in safety.
The High God surrounds him all day long,
and dwells between his shoulders."
DEUTERONOMY 33:12 ESV

It's middle-of-the-night late and I awake suddenly to a loud noise. My anxiety skyrockets when I reach for my husband and remember he is away on a business trip, and I am alone to face the nameless noise-maker.

By instinct I creep to the kids' rooms across the hall. Peeking around the boys' door, my heart skips upon seeing a dark mass on the ground. However, it relaxes considerably when I realize it is a pillow and a thick children's encyclopedia that had not been on the hardwood floor when I tucked them in. My elder son on the top bunk, active even in sleep, must have jostled it off. Mysterious noise-maker located.

Climbing back into bed, I recall a quote from Dallas Willard: "The promise is not that God will never allow any evil to come to us but that no matter what befalls us, we are still beyond genuine harm due to the fact that He remains with us." I inhale slowly and breathe out a prayer of gratitude to the God whose presence ensures my safety.

* * * * * * * * *

Ever-present Father, remind me of Your nearness when
I am anxious. Whatever comes, I am with You always.

SLIPPINGS AND STRAYINGS
THERE WILL BE, NO DOUBT,
BUT THE EVERLASTING ARMS
ARE BENEATH US;
WE SHALL BE CAUGHT,
RESCUED, RESTORED.

J. I. PACKER

PEACE IN CHAOS

Now may the Lord of peace himself give you peace at all times and in every way. The Lord be with all of you.

2 THESSALONIANS 3:16 NIV

Chaos seems to follow me like a lost puppy. It shows up as a sick child at the wrong time, or a lost job in the midst of new beginnings, or a lost parent during a child's rebellion and a move all at the same time. I must be a chaos magnet and as I grow older the magnet seems to get stronger. But chaos, unlike a cute puppy, is not a welcome visitor in my life.

The chaos may manifest in different ways but my peace always remains the same. God is a constant companion of mine and He is consistent. In a moment's time, my day can go sideways and God can set me back upright with one Scripture from His amazing Word.

Because I trust in Him, I can always know that in everything, at all times, in every way, His peace is assured and in His peace I am secure.

Father God, Your peace is all I need. I trust in You to provide the peace that surpasses all understanding at all times in my life. When chaos comes, cover me in Your peace.

THE PERFECT HOUSE

The Lord said to her, "My dear Martha, you are worried
and upset over all these details! There is only one thing
worth being concerned about. Mary has discovered it,
and it will not be taken away from her."

LUKE 10:41–42 NLT

ospitality was an important part of the biblical world, even as it is today.
Jesus mentions it often, in such stories as that of the Good Samaritan. We
need to remember that in the above passage, Jesus isn't criticizing Martha for
her work in making the disciples welcome. Instead, He's pointing out that she's
being distracted at that moment from what's more vital—hearing His words and
treasuring His presence.

In today's world, we often feel a crushing pressure to make our homes "perfect." Spotless. Uncluttered. Tastefully decorated. And there's certainly nothing wrong with keeping a house tidy.

But hospitality is more than a clean house. It's providing a welcome place for people to gather and enjoy each other's company. It's sharing your love of God as well as a good meal. It's an open heart as well as an open hearth.

If your spirit is welcoming, if you cherish those around you, the dust bunnies can wait.

* * * * * * * * *

Lord, show me how to share Your love. Open my heart to those around me, so I can welcome them into my home. Amen.

HOT PINK ASSURANCE

> Your Father knows exactly what you need
> even before you ask him!
> MATTHEW 6:8 NLT

Hurrying, attempting to stay one step ahead of the packers, my foot caught on something solid. I was catapulted forward, and a battle for balance ensued between gravity, the plant I was holding, and me. Gravity won…

My favorite plant, its bare roots hanging out, looked like I felt. I was exhausted, overwhelmed, and about to break under the "last straw" when my daughter's joyful appearance kept me from indulging in a mini-meltdown.

"Look, Mommy! Look!" she said, holding up a long-lost beach bucket.

"It was under the bed all along. You can use it if you want to. The mister-man said you might need it."

Indeed I did, and for a far more important reason than a makeshift planter. That pail was hot pink proof God knew and cared about everything I was going through during this move to a new duty station, and I needed that reassurance.

In stressful times, moving being one of the greatest, it helps to remember that even before we ask, God knows our every need—body, soul, and spirit. He cares about all the big and little things, including the occasional need for a hot pink beach bucket planter.

*Thank You, Creator Jesus, for intimately knowing
and caring about my every need.*

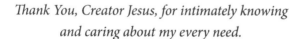

HIS PEACE WILL KEEP YOUR THOUGHTS AND YOUR HEARTS QUIET AND AT REST.

PHLIPPIANS 4:7 TLB